Finger Weaving Scarves & Wraps

Finger Weaving Scarves & Wraps
First published in the United States in 2015 by STACKPOLE BOOKS
5067 Ritter Road, Mechanicsburg, PA 17055
www.stackpolebooks.com

ISBN: 978-0-8117-1557-7

YUBIORI DE TSUKURU MUFFLER & SHAWL
Copyright © 2013 by Naoko Minowa
Originally published in Japanese language by Kawade Shobo Shinsha Ltd. Publishers
English translation rights arranged with Kawade Shobo Shinsha Ltd. Publishers through Timo
Associates, Inc., Tokyo
English language rights, translation & production by World Book Media, LLC
Email: info@worldbookmedia.com

English Translation: Kyoko Matthews
English Language Editor: Lindsay Fair
Designer: Michele L. Trombley
Cover Designer: Tessa J. Sweigert

Printed in China
10 9 8 7 6 5 4 3 2 1

Finger Weaving Scarves & Wraps

18 FUN, EASY PROJECTS
MADE WITHOUT LOOM, NEEDLE OR HOOK

NAOKO MINOWA

STACKPOLE
BOOKS

Introduction

When they hear the word weaving, many people are intimidated, imagining a large, noisy machine and hundreds of threads. But what if it was possible to weave without using a loom? What if your fingers were the only tools you needed to create beautiful scarves and wraps?

I have developed a simple finger weaving technique to make this dream possible. Now, everyone can experience the joy that comes from creating fabric with your very own hands.

The basic principles of finger weaving are the same as traditional hand weaving, but with finger weaving, the warp yarns are used in place of the weft yarns since there is no loom. Finger weaving also allows you to use a great variety of yarn, including soft, loosely twisted yarns that normally cannot be used on looms.

This book presents three different techniques for finger weaving. Use these methods to weave one of the 18 stylish projects included in this book. Once you understand the weaving process, you can alter the position of the yarn to create your own unique designs. In addition to scarves and wraps, you can weave your own bags, blankets, coasters, and other accessories.

Welcome to the world of weaving!

—Naoko Minowa

Contents

Romantic Ribbon Scarf

This scarf is woven using a wide, lacy
yarn to create a soft impression. Braided
fringe adds a feminine finishing touch.
For a fun twist, try combining two
scarves, as shown here.

Instructions on page 58

Herringbone Shawl

This lightweight wrap was created with the same type of yarn used for the Romantic Ribbon Scarf featured on the opposite page. Use two contrasting colors of yarn to accentuate the herringbone pattern.

Instructions on page 60

Checkered Scarf

This fashion-forward scarf design features a bold
checkered pattern. Black and white make a classic
combination, but this style works well in many colors.

Instructions on page 62

Alternate view of the Checkered Scarf from page 8

Houndstooth Scarf

The Houndstooth Scarf uses the same yarn and weaving technique as the Checkered Scarf featured on the opposite page. The classic houndstooth pattern is created by arranging the yarn in a different order before weaving.

Instructions on page 64

Simple Scarf

If you are new to finger weaving, this is the perfect project to start off with since it uses the Basic Weaving Technique. This simple, classic design works up quickly and is suitable for men and women alike.

Instructions on page 66

Textured Novelty Yarn Pillow

Update any room in your house with this fun and cheerful pillow. This project may look complicated, but it's actually quite simple to make; just combine fur novelty yarn with smooth super bulky yarn, then weave using the same basic technique used for the Simple Scarf on the opposite page.

Instructions on page 68

Chunky Confetti Scarf

Use a fun print yarn to add dimension to a simply woven scarf. Because this project is made with voluminous tube yarn, it requires less yarn than most scarf designs.

Instructions on page 70

Kid's Looped Neck Warmer

This miniature scarf packs a punch! In addition to keeping your little one's neck warm, it will also bring a smile to their face. This project takes only half an hour to create, so why not make it in a couple different colors?

Instructions on page 72

Chenille Fur Scarf

This versatile scarf works well with just about any outfit, especially when woven in a neutral color, such as the gray or white shown here. Combine faux fur chenille yarn with bulky-weight smooth yarn for a soft finish.

Instructions on page 74

Fiesta Fringe Shawl

A multicolored slub yarn provides this shawl with its unique uneven texture. This design is constructed using the Link Weaving Technique, which stretches vertically and allows for a comfortable fit when draped across your shoulders. Finish with coiled fringe in alternating colors of yarn to add even more cheer to this festive accessory.

Instructions on page 76

Stashbuster Scarf

This scarf provides the perfect opportunity to use up those leftover skeins of yarn you have lying around. Combine 10 strands of worsted-weight yarn to create a thick yarn suitable for finger weaving.

Instructions on page 78

Cat Nap Lap Blanket

This lap-sized blanket uses the same colors of yarn as the Stashbuster Scarf featured on the opposite page, just in different ratios. It's fun to watch the colors interact as you weave.

Instructions on page 80

Cross Weave Purse and Neck Warmer

Update your winter wardrobe with this matching set. To make the purse, simply attach the yarn to the handles and start weaving; you'll connect the sides and bottom later.

Instructions on pages 82–85

Classic Argyle Shawl

Use the Link Weaving Technique to create the traditional argyle pattern featured in this breathtaking shawl. This design is a bit time-consuming since it uses several strands of yarn, but the finished product is well worth the effort!

Instructions on page 86

Midnight
Sky Stole

Combine a variety of
dark-hued novelty yarns
to replicate the colors and
textures of a night sky.
This elegant accessory
is perfect for evening
ensembles.

Instructions on page 88

Beaded Bouclé Scarf

This lightweight scarf features soft bouclé yarn randomly interspersed with beads. The colorful beads add a bit of glamour to the naturally-textured yarn, creating an overall modern look.

Instructions on page 90

Sweet Summer Scarves

Created from cotton tape yarn, these airy and delicate scarves are designed for warmer weather. Instructions are included for both a narrow and a wide variation.

Instructions on page 92

Striped Sunset Afghan

The Basic Weaving Technique is used to accentuate the striped lines of this design. Made from tube yarn, this lightweight blanket is perfect for warming up on chilly spring days.

Instructions on page 94

Textured Lattice Scarf

This scarf combines faux fur yarn with smooth yarn to create a three-dimensional diamond design. Use contrasting colors, such as the brown and white pictured here, for a bold look.

Instructions on page 96

Before You Begin

Tools & Materials

Finger weaving does not require a lot of special equipment. In fact, you may already have everything you need to get started! Here are a few items you'll need to complete the projects included in this book.

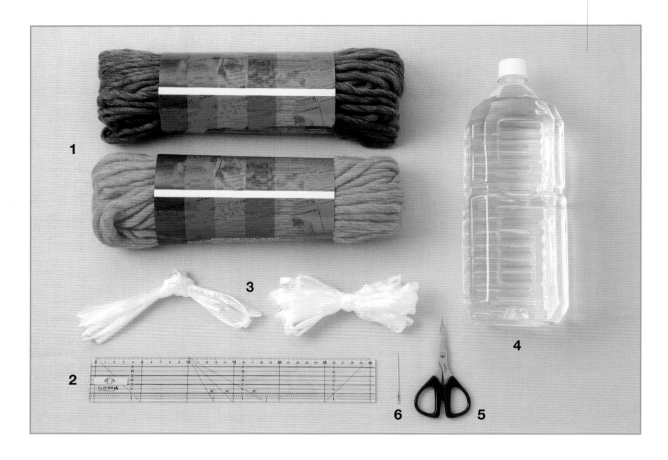

1. YARN: Super bulky yarn is recommended to achieve the chunky look of the designs included in this book. You can also combine multiple strands of medium-weight yarn, as shown on page 30.

2. RULER: Attach the yarn to a ruler to anchor the work while weaving. Depending on the size of the project, a 12" (30 cm) or 20" (50 cm) long ruler will work well.

3. STRING: Tie a 59" (150 cm) long piece of packing string to the ruler to hold it in place as you work, as shown on page 32. Use a 19 ¾"-39 ½" (50-100 cm) long piece of packing string or other smooth, medium-weight string as a temporary placeholder to prevent unraveling, as shown on page 34.

4. WATER BOTTLE: Place a full 2L square plastic water bottle on top of the string, as shown on page 32. The water bottle will act as a weight and hold the ruler firmly in place as you work.

5. SCISSORS: Designate a pair of scissors to be used for cutting yarn only.

6. NEEDLE: Use a large needle to finish fringe and join woven pieces together.

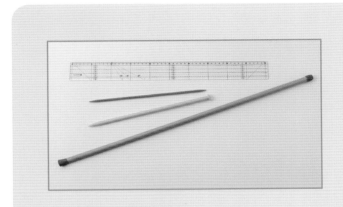

Instead of using a ruler, you can also use a thick knitting needle or a tension rod to anchor your yarn.

OTHER USEFUL TOOLS

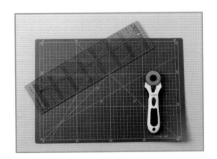

You may find it worthwhile to invest in a few additional tools for making fringe. Use a cutting mat, rotary cutter, and bias tape cutting ruler to trim fringe more quickly and easily than using scissors.

Insert the blade of the cutter into the groove of the bias tape cutting ruler. This will allow for a nice even cut since the yarn is secured in place by the ruler.

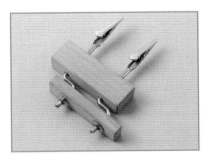

Instead of twisting the yarn between your fingers, use a fringe twister to create professionally finished fringe. Refer to page 56 for instructions on making fringe using this tool.

TUBE YARN: This type of yarn is loosely knitted into a tube. Its wide diameter and soft, lightweight texture make this yarn easy to handle.

SUPER BULKY YARN: These are the thickest yarns according to the standard yarn weight system. Super bulky yarn is available in a wide variety of colors.

TAPE YARN: This flat, woven yarn is also known as ribbon yarn. When finger weaving, look for 1 ¼"-2" (3-5 cm) wide tape yarn.

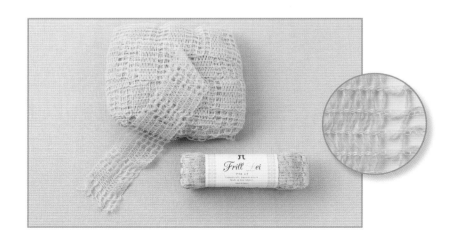

NOVELTY YARN: There is a wide assortment of novelty yarn available in today's market, including slub yarn and fur yarn. Although fur yarn has a thin core, the fluffy bits increase its overall width, making it suitable for use in finger weaving.

FABRIC YARN: Create your own yarn by tearing or cutting fleece or chiffon into ¾"-2" (2-5 cm) wide strips.

Preparing Fabric Yarn

When making strips from fleece, always cut the fleece along the cross-grain, which is the direction with the most stretch. After cutting the strips, pull to curl the fabric into a thick, round tube. This will make the fleece easy to handle while weaving.

MULTIPLE STRAND YARN:

Combine about 10 strands of medium-weight yarn to create a weaving yarn that is about ¾" (2 cm) wide. This is a great use for leftover yarn.

Preparing the Multiple Strand Yarn

Roll multiple yarns into one ball to create a thicker yarn suitable for finger weaving.

If you run out of yarn while weaving, simply tie another piece onto the end. Since this type of yarn creates a variegated effect, it won't matter if you attach pieces that are different colors.

Getting Started

Before you jump right into a project, take a few minutes to set up properly. Preparing your yarn, selecting the best starting method for your project, and taking steps to prevent your work from unraveling will save time and frustration in the long run!

STEP 1: PREPARE YOUR YARN

Yarn is sometimes sold in hanks, which need to be wound into a ball before use in order to prevent tangling. Before starting your finger weaving project, always wind the yarn into a ball, then cut the necessary number of pieces.

1. Wind the hank of yarn into a ball.

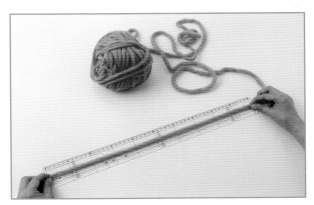

2. Measure and cut the pieces of yarn to the specified length.

Note: *Rather than measuring out each piece of yarn individually, you can use the first piece of yarn you cut as a guide for measuring the others.*

LOOP START METHOD

This method requires you to cut long pieces of yarn that will be folded in half when attached to the ruler. Always use this method when a project calls for the fringe to be finished with a Braided Loop (see page 52).

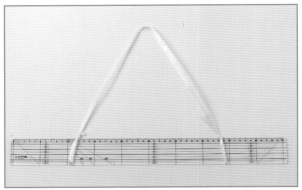

1. Tie a 59" (150 cm) long string to both ends of the ruler.

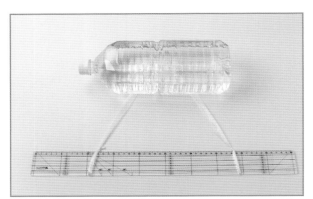

2. Pull the string taut at the center. Use a full plastic water bottle as a weight to hold the string and ruler in place.

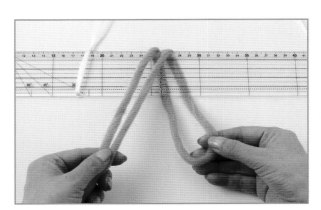

3. Fold one piece of yarn in half and bring the loop under the ruler.

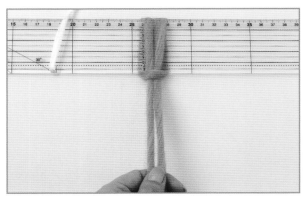

4. Insert both ends of the yarn through the loop and pull to bring the knot up to the edge of the ruler.

5. Repeat steps 3-4 to attach the remaining pieces of yarn to the ruler.

6. Completed view once all pieces of yarn have been attached to the ruler using the Loop Start Method.

SINGLE KNOT START METHOD

With this method, you'll cut each piece of yarn individually, then tie multiple pieces together to attach to the ruler. This method allows you to adjust the fringe length easily and is suitable for projects that use longer weaving yarns.

1. Arrange half of the yarn in front of the ruler and half in the back. Note: This example uses 4 pieces for each bundle, but the number of pieces will vary depending on the project design or yarn thickness.

2. Make a knot, leaving enough yarn above the knot as specified for the fringe length.

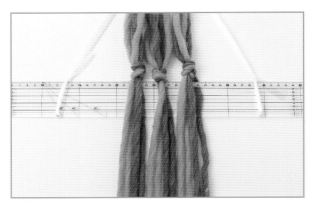

Note: When using multiple colors, pay attention to the order in which you arrange the yarn when attaching to the ruler as this will influence the finished pattern. Refer to the individual project instructions for specific order.

3. Follow the same process to attach the remaining pieces of yarn in bundles.

STEP 3: PREVENT YOUR WORK FROM UNRAVELING

When it's time to remove the ruler, your weaving may become loose and start to unravel. Follow this process to insert a temporary placeholder string through the first few rows to secure the weave. When using the Loop Start Method to create a project with long fringe, insert the string through several rows. This will you allow you to adjust the fringe length easily.

1. Pick up the left strand of each set attached to the ruler.

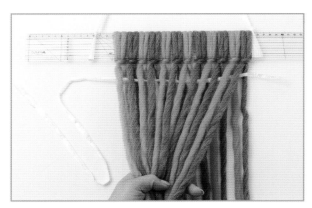

2. Insert a 19 ¾"-39 ½" (50-100 cm) long string between the two layers of yarn.

3. Pick up the right strand of each set attached to the ruler (these are the strands that made up the bottom layer in step 2).

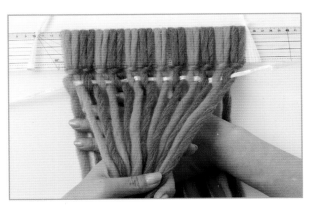

4. Lift these strands up while holding the new bottom layer of yarn down with your other hand.

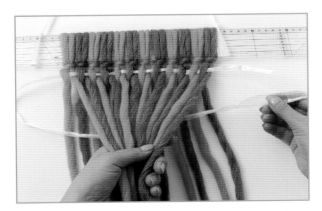

5. Insert the string between the two layers of yarn again.

6. Pick up the strands of yarn positioned under the string (these are the strands that made up the bottom layer in step 5).

7. Lift these strands up while holding the new bottom layer of yarn down with your other hand.

8. Insert the string between the two layers of yarn one more time. You are now ready to start weaving!

Follow the same process to prevent your work from unraveling when using the Single Knot Start Method.

Note: *When using multiple colors, pay attention to the order of the yarn as you insert the string as this will influence the finished pattern.*

Weaving Techniques

BASIC WEAVING TECHNIQUE

The Basic Weaving Technique uses the far left strand in each row as the weft (horizontal) yarn. This method produces a slanted, striped pattern when worked in two or more colors of yarn.

MATERIALS
- 20 yards (38 g) of super bulky-weight (#6 super bulky) wool yarn in orange
- 20 yards (38 g) of super bulky-weight (#6 super bulky) wool yarn in brown

GETTING STARTED

1. For each color, cut 6 pieces of yarn that measure 118 ¼" (300 cm) long each. You should have a total of 12 pieces of yarn.

2. Attach the yarn to the ruler using the Loop Start Method (see page 32). Make sure to alternate yarn colors as shown in the step 1 photo below. Once the yarn is attached to the ruler, there will be 24 strands of yarn that measure 59" (150 cm) long each. Insert a string through for three rows to prevent your work from unraveling (see page 34).

INSTRUCTIONS

1. Separate the far left strand to be used as the weft yarn.

2. Pick up the strands of yarn positioned under the third string (in this example, these are the right strings of each looped piece of yarn).

3. Lift these strands up while holding the bottom layer of yarn down with your other hand.

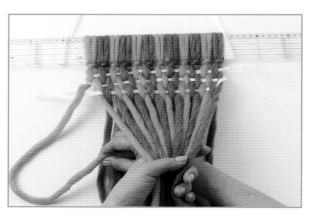

4. Insert the weft yarn between the two layers.

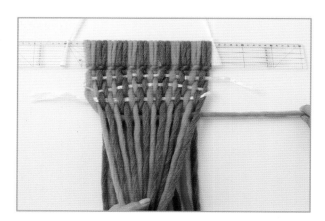

5. The first row is complete. Leave the weft yarn at the right edge for now—it will eventually become a warp (vertical) yarn.

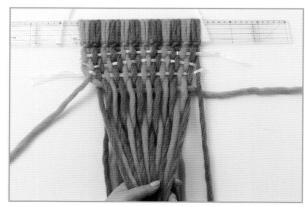

6. Separate the far left strand to be used as the new weft yarn. Pick up the strands of yarn that made up the bottom layer of the previous row.

When picking up the bottom layer of yarn, pull the strands taut to tighten the weft yarn and stabilize the weave.

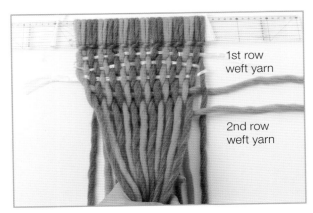

1st row weft yarn

2nd row weft yarn

7. Insert the weft yarn between the two layers following the same process used in step 4.

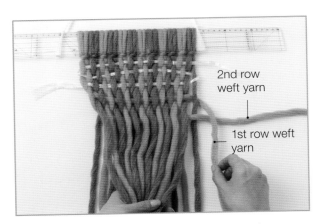

2nd row weft yarn

1st row weft yarn

8. Bring the first row weft yarn down so it becomes a warp yarn. Make sure it crosses over the second row weft yarn.

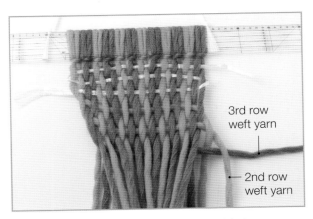

3rd row weft yarn

2nd row weft yarn

9. Repeat steps 6-7 to weave the third row. Bring the second row weft yarn down so it becomes a warp yarn again. Make sure it crosses over the third row weft yarn.

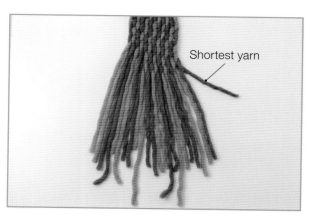

Shortest yarn

10. Continue weaving, making sure to always use the far left strand as the weft yarn. As you weave, move the plastic water bottle closer to you to hold the work in place.

11. The weaving process will cause the strands of yarn to become uneven in length. Weave until the shortest strand equals the desired fringe length (6"-8" [15-20 cm] in this example).

12. Finish the fringe (see page 51), or continue with steps 13-15 to level out the end of the weave before finishing the fringe.

13. The last row of weaving will be slanted, as visible in the step 11 photo above. To level out this row, separate the far left strand as the weft yarn. Pick up about half of the strands that made up the bottom layer of the previous row. Weave the weft yarn between the two layers. The weft yarn will be positioned in the middle of work.

14. Repeat step 13, but only weave the weft yarn through a quarter of the work this time.

15. The end of the work is now level.

Tips for Working with Multiple Strand Yarn

When attaching bundles of multiple strand yarn to the ruler, use rubber bands to hold each bundle together.

When weaving with multiple strand yarn, it is easiest to pick up each bundle by gripping the rubber band.

Other Ways to Use the Basic Weaving Technique

In addition to making scarves and shawls, you can also use the Basic Weaving Technique to create beautiful jewelry. Once you master the weaving technique, use the same process to make a variety of accessories.

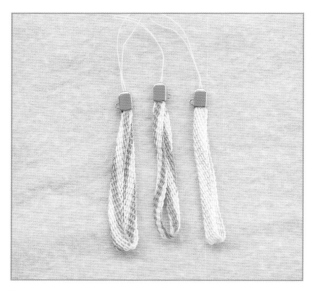

Use two contrasting colors of cotton thread to weave one-of-a-kind keychains.

Use 1.5 mm wide waxed cotton cord and gemstone beads to create these Bohemian-style bracelets.

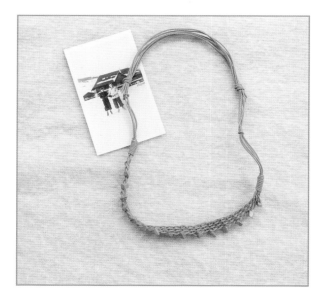

Use 1.5 mm wide waxed cotton cord and matching beads to weave this adjustable necklace.

Use 1.5 mm wide metallic gimp and clear gemstone beads to weave this lariat-style necklace.

CROSS WEAVING TECHNIQUE

With the Cross Weaving Technique, you'll divide the warp yarns into two groups, then weave using two crossed strands as the weft yarns. Since the cross method is very sturdy, it is recommended for projects that receive a lot of wear and tear, such as bags.

MATERIALS

- 20 yards (38 g) of super bulky-weight (#6 super bulky) wool yarn in orange
- 20 yards (38 g) of super bulky-weight (#6 super bulky) wool yarn in brown

GETTING STARTED

1. For each color, cut 6 pieces of yarn that measure 118 ¼" (300 cm) long each. You should have a total of 12 pieces of yarn.

2. Attach the yarn to the ruler using the Loop Start Method (see page 32). Once the yarn is attached to the ruler, there will be 24 strands of yarn that measure 59" (150 cm) long each. Insert a string through for three rows to prevent your work from unraveling (see page 34).

INSTRUCTIONS

1. Divide the yarn into two equal groups.

2. Cross the two center strands to use as the weft yarns. Make sure to cross the strand positioned under the third string on top, as shown by the orange strand in the above photo.

3. For the left side, pick up the strands of yarn positioned under the third string. Insert the bottom weft yarn (brown) between the two layers.

4. Follow the same process for the right side, but use the top weft yarn (orange). The first row is complete.

5. Cross the two new center strands to use as the weft yarns, just like in step 2.

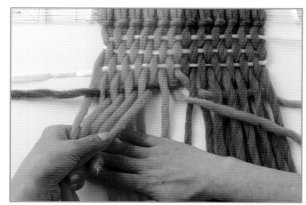

6. For the left side, pick up the strands of yarn that made up the bottom layer of the first row. Pull the strands taut to tighten the weave.

7. Insert the bottom weft yarn (brown) between the two layers. Follow the same process for the right side, but use the top weft yarn (orange). Bring the first row weft yarns down so they become warp yarns. Make sure the first row weft yarn crosses under the second row weft yarn on the left side and over the second row weft yarn on the right side.

8. Follow the same process to complete the third row.

9. Continue weaving until you reach desired length. This weaving technique will create an inverted V pattern.

10. To level out the end of the work, weave the weft yarn through half, then a quarter of the work for each side. This will fill in the middle of the work.

11. Finish the end fringe using necktie knots (see page 51). Finish the beginning fringe using the Braided Loop (see page 52).

LINK WEAVING TECHNIQUE

With the Link Weaving Technique, you'll separate the warp yarns into two layers and cross them over each other alternately as you weave. This method does not use a weft yarn, so it produces a weave that easily stretches vertically. This characteristic makes this technique ideal for loosely woven projects, such as blankets.

MATERIALS

- 20 yards (38 g) of super bulky-weight (#6 super bulky) wool yarn in orange
- 20 yards (38 g) of super bulky-weight (#6 super bulky) wool yarn in brown

GETTING STARTED

1. For each color, cut 6 pieces of yarn that measure 118 ¼" (300 cm) long each. You should have a total of 12 pieces of yarn.

2. Attach the yarn to the ruler using the Loop Start Method (see page 32). Make sure to alternate yarn colors as shown in the step 1 photo below. Once the yarn is attached to the ruler, there will be 24 strands of yarn that measure 59" (150 cm) long each. Insert a string through for three rows to prevent your work from unraveling (see page 34).

INSTRUCTIONS

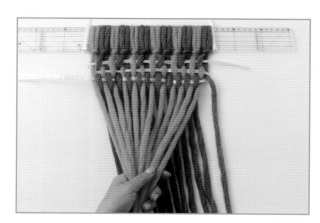

1. Separate the yarn positioned under the third string (orange in the above photo) from the yarn positioned over the third string (brown in the above photo).

2. Pick up the strands of yarn positioned under the third string (orange).

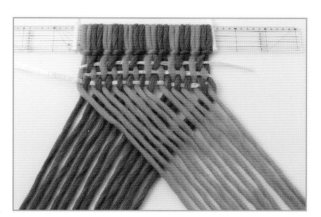

3. Arrange the picked-up strands (orange) on top of the strands positioned over the third string (brown). Position the orange yarn so it extends toward the bottom right and the brown yarn so it extends toward the bottom left. Keep the yarn positioned this way as you weave.

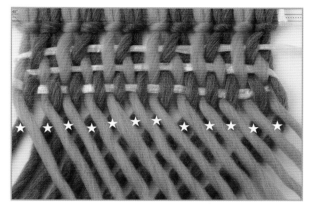

4. Pick up the new bottom layer of yarn (brown) at the points where the two colors of yarn overlap, as indicated by the ★s.

5. Make sure the brown yarn crosses under the orange yarn as you pick it up.

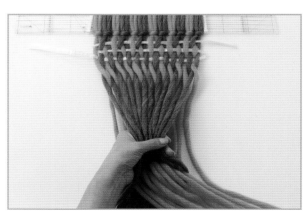

6. Lift up the brown yarn so it becomes the new top layer. Separate the brown yarn from the orange yarn.

7. After separating the two colors of yarn, arrange the strands in the same position used in step 3. Note: This time, the brown yarn will be on top of the orange yarn.

8. Pick up the new bottom layer of yarn (orange) at the points where the two colors of yarn overlap, as indicated by the ★s, just like in step 4.

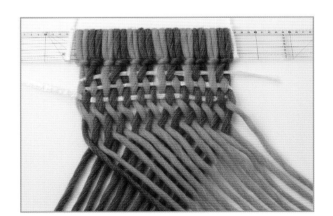

9. Lift up and separate the orange yarn so it becomes the new top layer. This new layer will also include the leftmost brown strand of yarn. Arrange the orange yarn on top of the brown yarn.

10. Repeat steps 4-7 to arrange the brown yarn (plus the rightmost orange strand) on top of the orange yarn. Completed view of 4 rows.

11. Completed view of 12 rows. The Link Weaving Technique always results in a level edge. Note: The yarn will return to its original position after 24 rows have been completed.

12. Finish the end fringe using necktie knots (see page 51) and the beginning fringe using the Braided Loop (see page 52).

CENTER START METHOD

The Link Weaving Technique requires you to separate the two layers of yarn for every row you weave. This can be difficult, especially when a project requires you to use long strands of yarn. The following guide shows you how to start weaving from the center of the work using only half the length of yarn at one time. This method can also be used with the Basic Weaving Technique.

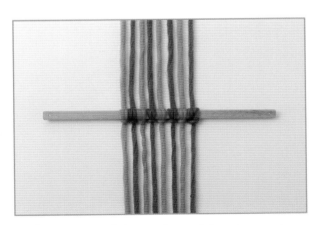

1. Attach the yarn to the ruler using the Loop Start Method (see page 32). As always with this method, you will have twice the number of strands once the yarn has been attached to the ruler.

2. Separate each loop of yarn into a top and bottom strand.

3. Weave the bottom strands using the Link Weaving Technique as shown on pages 46–49. Do not insert a string through to prevent the work from unraveling. When you reach the desired length, finish the fringe as desired.

4. Remove the ruler.

5. Untie the knots used to attach the yarn to the ruler.

6. Rotate the work so the woven section is positioned at the top. Weave the remaining half and finish the fringe as desired.

Finishing Methods

Once you finish weaving, use these options to finish both ends of the work. Note that certain finishing methods can only be used in conjunction with a particular start method.

A. THE NECKTIE KNOT

SINGLE

1. When the weaving is complete, hold the weft yarn from the final row in your right hand and the rest of the yarn in your left hand. Wrap the weft yarn around the bundle in your left hand one time.

2. Bring the weft yarn through the loop to tighten.

3. Pull the knot taut. Trim the fringe to desired length.

MULTIPLE

1. After finishing the fringe at the end of the work, position the work so the starting edge is closest to you.

2. Remove the ruler and untie the knots.

3. Starting from the center, cut the string used to prevent your work from unraveling.

Note: If you prefer an even finish, refer to pages 40–41 to level out the end of the weave before completing steps 4 and 5.

4. Remove the string from the right half of the work. Finish the fringe with necktie knots (see page 51). This example uses four strands of yarn per bundle.

5. Remove the string from the left half of the work and finish the fringe with necktie knots.

B. THE BRAIDED LOOP

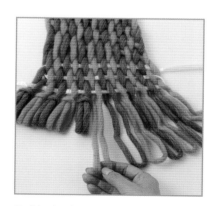

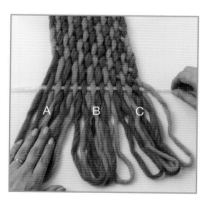

1. Position the work so the starting edge is closest to you. Remove the ruler.

2. Untie the knots used to attach the yarn to the ruler.

3. Remove the string used to prevent your work from unraveling. Divide the yarn loops into three groups: A, B, and C.

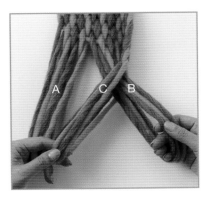

4. Insert group B through the loops of group C.

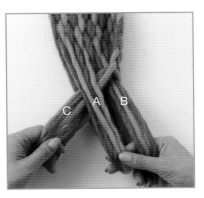

5. Insert group C through the loops of group A.

6. Insert group A through the loops of group B.

7. Insert group B through the loops of group C.

8. Follow the same process to continue braiding until you reach the end of the yarn.

9. Completed view of the braid.

10. Insert a small, thin scrap of yarn through all of the loops and tie a knot. Note: A contrasting color of yarn is used here for visual clarity. Use a scrap of yarn in a coordinating color to your project so the knot isn't visible.

11. Completed view of the knot.

12. Use a tapestry needle to weave the yarn tails into the braid. Trim the excess yarn.

C. COILED FRINGE

1. Bundle two strands of yarn together and tie a necktie knot (see page 51). Follow the same process for all remaining strands of yarn.

2. Tie three bundles together using a scrap of yarn.

3. Wrap the scrap of yarn around the bundle to form a coil.

4. When the coil has reached the desired size, insert the yarn tail through the final loop and tighten (this is the same process as the necktie knot).

5. Use a tapestry needle to weave both yarn tails through the coil.

6. Trim the excess yarn.

D. TWISTED FRINGE

BY HAND

1. Twist a few strands of yarn together (as shown by the maroon yarn in the above photo).

2. While holding the twisted bundle from step 1 in one hand, twist another bundle of yarn using your other hand (as shown by the white yarn in the above photo). Make sure to twist in same direction as step 1.

3. Twist the two bundles together, making sure to twist in the opposite direction of steps 1 and 2. Secure with a necktie knot (see page 51).

USING A FRINGE TWISTER

1. Clip two bundles of yarn to the fringe twister. Rotate the handle to twist the bundles.

2. Join the twisted bundles together with one clip. Rotate the handle in the opposite direction of step 1 to twist the two bundles together.

3. Completed view of the twisted fringe. The fringe twister allows you to twist fringe more tightly than when using your fingers.

E. BRAIDS

1. Divide the strands of yarn into three groups. Note: For this example, the yarn was divided in half prior to being divided in three groups.

2. Braid the three groups of yarn.

3. Finish the braid with a necktie knot (see page 51). Trim the excess yarn.

Project Instructions

Romantic Ribbon Scarf

Shown on page 6

MATERIALS

- 50 yards (90 g) of bulky-weight (#5 bulky) acrylic/nylon blend tape yarn in pink or white

GAUGE

- 4 weft yarns = 4" (10 cm)

GETTING STARTED

1. Cut 18 pieces of yarn that measure 98 ½" (250 cm) long each.

2. Attach the yarn to the ruler using the Single Knot Start Method (see page 33). Use 2 pieces of yarn for each bundle. Insert a string through for two rows to prevent your work from unraveling.

INSTRUCTIONS

1. Weave using the Cross Weaving Technique (see page 43) until the work measures 59" (150 cm) long.

2. Finish the fringe on both ends of the scarf by braiding (see page 56). Refer to the project diagram on page 59 for details on creating the fringe.

PROJECT DIAGRAM

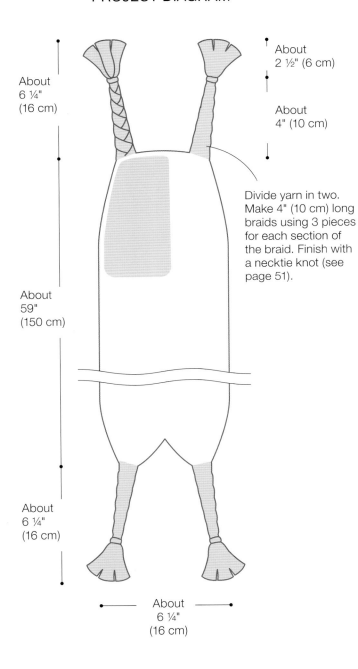

About
2 ½" (6 cm)

About
4" (10 cm)

About
6 ¼"
(16 cm)

Divide yarn in two.
Make 4" (10 cm) long
braids using 3 pieces
for each section of
the braid. Finish with
a necktie knot (see
page 51).

About
59"
(150 cm)

About
6 ¼"
(16 cm)

About
6 ¼"
(16 cm)

Herringbone Shawl

Shown on page 7

MATERIALS

- 66 yards (120 g) of bulky-weight (#5 bulky) acrylic/nylon blend tape yarn in beige
- 66 yards (120 g) of bulky-weight (#5 bulky) acrylic/nylon blend tape yarn in dark brown

GAUGE

- 4 weft yarns = 4" (10 cm)

GETTING STARTED

1. For each color, cut 24 pieces of yarn that measure 98 ½" (250 cm) long each. You should have a total of 48 pieces of yarn.

2. Attach the yarn to the ruler using the Single Knot Start Method (see page 33). Use 6 pieces of yarn for each bundle. Refer to the photo below for yarn color order. Insert a string through for two rows to prevent your work from unraveling.

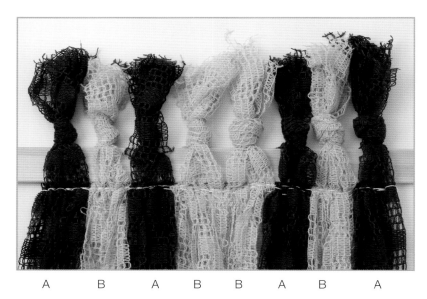

A	B	A	B	B	A	B	A

A: 6 pieces of dark brown tape yarn
B: 6 pieces of beige tape yarn

INSTRUCTIONS

1. Weave using the Cross Weaving Technique (see page 43) until the work measures 51 ¼" (130 cm) long.

2. Finish the fringe on both ends of the shawl using necktie knots (see page 51). Refer to the project diagram below for details on creating the fringe.

PROJECT DIAGRAM

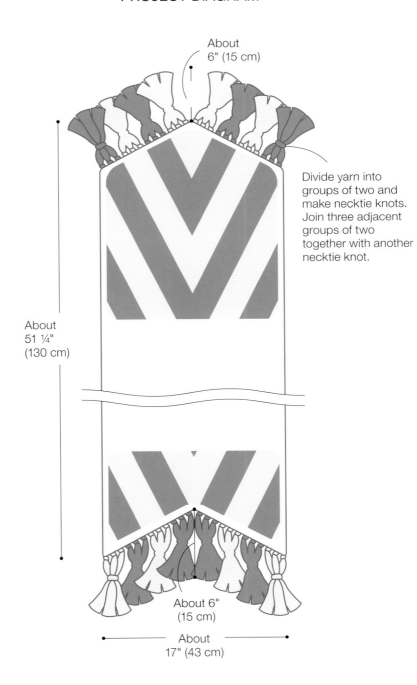

About 6" (15 cm)

Divide yarn into groups of two and make necktie knots. Join three adjacent groups of two together with another necktie knot.

About 51 ¼" (130 cm)

About 6" (15 cm)

About 17" (43 cm)

Checkered Scarf

Shown on page 8

MATERIALS

- 44 yards (84 g) of super bulky-weight (#6 super bulky) wool yarn in black
- 44 yards (84 g) of super bulky-weight (#6 super bulky) wool yarn in white

GAUGE

- 6 weft yarns = 4" (10 cm)

GETTING STARTED

1. For each color, cut 8 pieces of yarn that measure 197" (500 cm) long each. You should have a total of 16 pieces of yarn.

2. Attach the yarn to the ruler using the Loop Start Method (see page 32). Refer to the photo below for yarn color order. Once the yarn is attached to the ruler, there will be 32 strands of yarn that measure 98 ½" (250 cm) long each. Insert a string through for three rows to prevent your work from unraveling (see page 34).

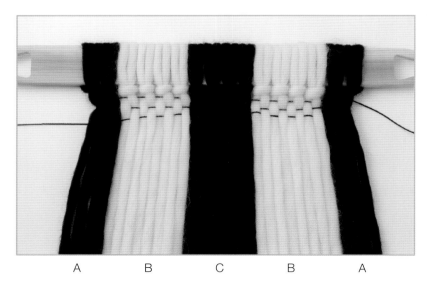

A: 2 pieces of black wool yarn
B: 4 pieces of white wool yarn
C: 4 pieces of black wool yarn

INSTRUCTIONS

1. Weave using the Link Weaving Technique (see page 46) until the work measures 61" (155 cm) long.

2. Finish the fringe on both ends of the scarf using necktie knots (see page 51). Refer to the project diagram below for details on creating the fringe.

PROJECT DIAGRAM

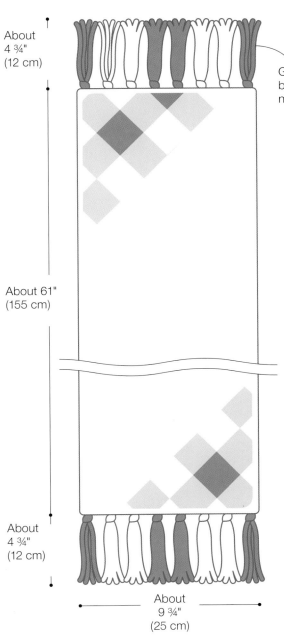

About 4 ¾" (12 cm)

Group yarn into bundles of 4 using necktie knots.

About 61" (155 cm)

About 4 ¾" (12 cm)

About 9 ¾" (25 cm)

Note: You can also use the Single Knot Start Method (see page 33) or the Center Start Method (see page 49) for this project. To use either method, cut 16 pieces of each color yarn that measure 98 ½" (250 cm) long each.

Houndstooth Scarf

Shown on page 9

MATERIALS

- 44 yards (84 g) of super bulky-weight (#6 super bulky) wool yarn in black
- 44 yards (84 g) of super bulky-weight wool yarn (#6 super bulky) wool in white

GAUGE

- 6 weft yarns = 4" (10 cm)

GETTING STARTED

1. For each color, cut 8 pieces of yarn that measure 197" (500 cm) long each. You should have a total of 16 pieces of yarn.

2. Attach the yarn to the ruler using the Loop Start Method (see page 32). Refer to the photo below for yarn color order. Once the yarn is attached to the ruler, there will be 32 strands of yarn that measure 98 ½" (250 cm) long each. Insert a string through for three rows to prevent your work from unraveling (see page 34).

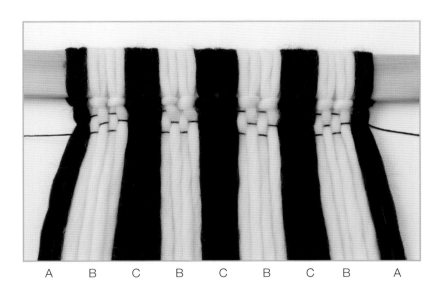

A   B   C   B   C   B   C   B   A

A: 1 piece of black wool yarn
B: 2 pieces of white wool yarn
C: 2 pieces of black wool yarn

INSTRUCTIONS

1. Weave using the Link Weaving Technique (see page 46) until the work measures 61" (155 cm) long.

2. Finish the fringe on both ends of the scarf using necktie knots (see page 51). Refer to the project diagram below for details on creating the fringe.

PROJECT DIAGRAM

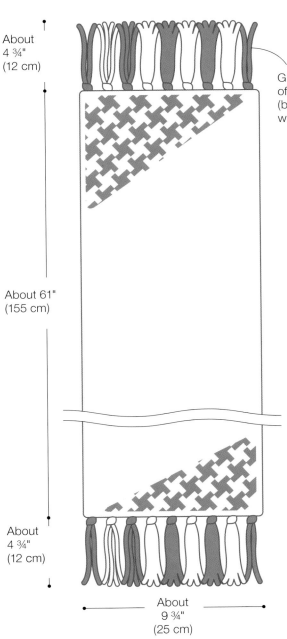

About
4 ¾"
(12 cm)

Group yarn into bundles
of 4 using necktie knots
(bundles on the ends
will have 2 pieces each).

About 61"
(155 cm)

About
4 ¾"
(12 cm)

About
9 ¾"
(25 cm)

> **Note:** *You can also use the Single Knot Start Method (see page 33) or the Center Start Method (see page 49) for this project. To use either method, cut 16 pieces of each color yarn that measure 98 ½" (250 cm) long each.*

Simple Scarf

Shown on page 10

MATERIALS

- 99 yards (188 g) of super bulky-weight (#6 super bulky) wool yarn in teal

GAUGE

- 3 weft yarns = 4" (10 cm)

GETTING STARTED

1. Cut 36 pieces of yarn that measure 98 ½" (250 cm) long each.

2. Attach the yarn to the ruler using the Single Knot Start Method (see page 33). Use 4 pieces of yarn for each bundle. Insert a string through for three rows to prevent your work from unraveling (see page 34).

A: 4 pieces of wool yarn

INSTRUCTIONS

1. Weave using the Basic Weaving Technique (see page 37) until the work measures 55" (140 cm) long.

2. Finish the fringe on both ends of the scarf using necktie knots (see page 51). Refer to the project diagram below for details on creating the fringe.

PROJECT DIAGRAM

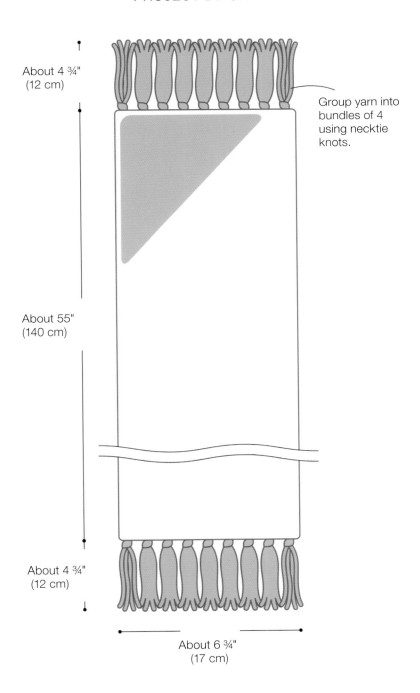

About 4 ¾"
(12 cm)

Group yarn into
bundles of 4
using necktie
knots.

About 55"
(140 cm)

About 4 ¾"
(12 cm)

About 6 ¾"
(17 cm)

Textured Novelty Yarn Pillow

Shown on page 11

MATERIALS

- 99 yards (157 g) of bulky-weight (#5 bulky) wool/acrylic blend fur yarn in variegated blue/purple
- 197 yards (206 g) of super bulky-weight (#6 super bulky) wool/acrylic blend smooth yarn in periwinkle
- Polyester/cotton stuffing
- 60 small rubber bands

GAUGE

- 5 weft yarns = 4" (10 cm)

GETTING STARTED

1. Combine 1 strand of fur yarn and 2 strands of smooth yarn and roll into a ball to create multiple strand yarn.

2. Cut 30 pieces of multiple strand yarn that measure 118 ¼" (300 cm) long each.

3. Attach the yarn to the ruler using the Loop Start Method (see page 32). Use rubber bands to hold each 3 strand bundle together as shown on page 41. Once the yarn is attached to the ruler, there will be 60 bundles of yarn that measure 59" (150 cm) long each. Insert a string through for three rows to prevent your work from unraveling (see page 34).

Multiple strand yarn ratio

A: 1 piece of fur yarn + 2 pieces of smooth yarn

INSTRUCTIONS

1. Weave using the Basic Weaving Technique (see page 37) until the work measures 21 ¼" (54 cm) long.

2. Join the bundles of fringe to the starting edge loops using necktie knots (see page 51). This will form the woven piece into a tube.

3. Turn the tube inside out. Pull the strands of yarn through to the wrong side. Insert the stuffing and sew the sides of the pillow closed using a scrap of smooth yarn.

Tie the fringe to the starting edge loops.

Sew the sides of the pillow closed.

PROJECT DIAGRAM

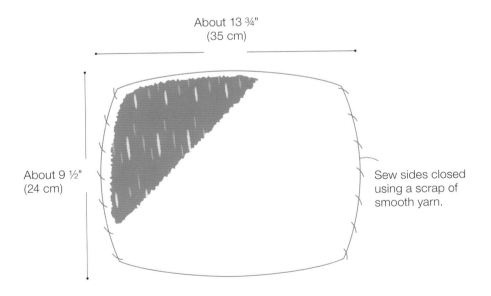

About 13 ¾"
(35 cm)

About 9 ½"
(24 cm)

Sew sides closed using a scrap of smooth yarn.

Chunky Confetti Scarf

Shown on page 12

MATERIALS

- 66 yards (167 g) of bulky-weight (#5 bulky) wool/nylon blend tube yarn in variegated white

GAUGE

- 4 weft yarns = 4" (10 cm)

GETTING STARTED

1. Cut 24 pieces of yarn that measure 98 ½" (250 cm) long each.

2. Attach the yarn to the ruler using the Single Knot Start Method (see page 33). Use 4 pieces of yarn for each bundle. Insert a string through for three rows to prevent your work from unraveling (see page 34).

INSTRUCTIONS

1. Weave using the Cross Weaving Technique (see page 43) until the work measures 55" (140 cm) long.

2. Finish the fringe on both ends of the scarf using necktie knots (see page 51). Refer to the project diagram on page 71 for details on creating the fringe.

Note: Because tube yarn is flat, it can twist during the weaving process. Take care not to twist the yarn as this will create undesirable gaps in the weave.

PROJECT DIAGRAM

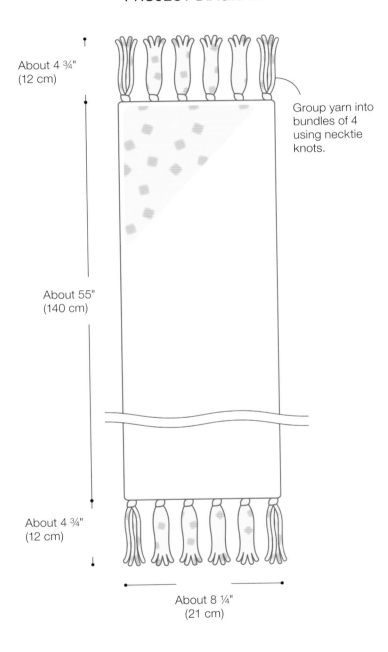

About 4 ¾"
(12 cm)

Group yarn into
bundles of 4
using necktie
knots.

About 55"
(140 cm)

About 4 ¾"
(12 cm)

About 8 ¼"
(21 cm)

Kid's Looped Neck Warmer

Shown on page 13

MATERIALS

- 33 yards (84 g) of bulky-weight (#5 bulky) wool/nylon blend tube yarn in variegated pink or gray

GAUGE

- 4 weft yarns = 4" (10 cm)

GETTING STARTED

1. Cut 10 pieces of yarn that measure 118 ¼" (300 cm) long each.

2. Attach the yarn to the ruler using the Loop Start Method (see page 32). Once the yarn is attached to the ruler, there will be 20 strands of yarn that measure 59" (150 cm) long each. Insert a string through for three rows to prevent your work from unraveling (see page 34).

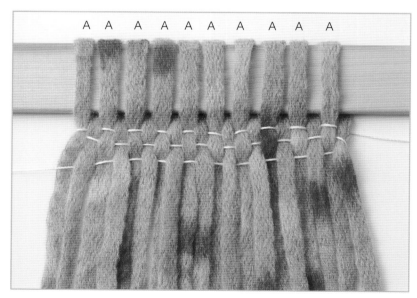

A: 1 piece of tube yarn

INSTRUCTIONS

1. Weave using the Cross Weaving Technique (see page 43) until the work measures 19" (48 cm) long.

2. Finish the end fringe using a necktie knot (see page 51) and the beginning fringe using the Braided Loop (see page 52). Refer to the project diagram below for details on creating the fringe.

Note: *Because tube yarn is flat, it can twist during the weaving process. Take care not to twist the yarn as this will create undesirable gaps in the weave.*

PROJECT DIAGRAM

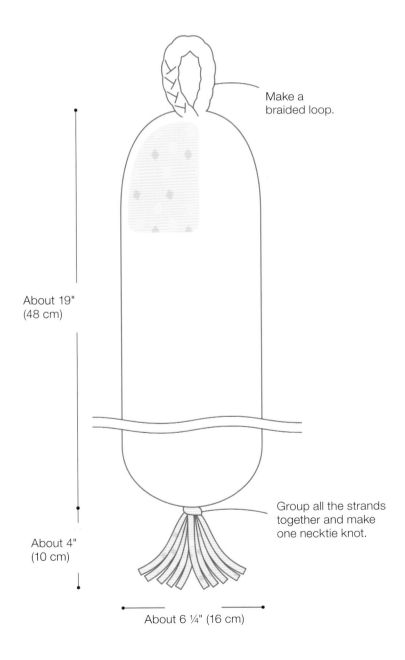

Make a braided loop.

About 19" (48 cm)

Group all the strands together and make one necktie knot.

About 4" (10 cm)

About 6 ¼" (16 cm)

Chenille Fur Scarf

Shown on page 14

MATERIALS

- 44 yards (100 g) of super bulky-weight (#6 super bulky) wool/acrylic blend faux fur chenille yarn in white or gray
- 44 yards (46 g) of bulky-weight (#5 bulky) wool/acrylic blend smooth yarn in white or gray

GAUGE

- 8 weft yarns = 4" (10 cm)

GETTING STARTED

1. For each type of yarn, cut 16 pieces of yarn that measure 98 ½" (250 cm) long each. You should have a total of 32 pieces of yarn.

2. Attach the yarn to the ruler using the Single Knot Start Method (see page 33). Use 2 pieces of fur yarn and 2 pieces of smooth yarn for each bundle. Insert a string through for three rows to prevent your work from unraveling (see page 34). When inserting the string, alternate the type of yarn positioned over the string for each row.

A: 2 pieces of faux fur chenille yarn + 2 pieces of smooth yarn

INSTRUCTIONS

1. Weave using the Basic Weaving Technique (see page 37) until the work measures 59" (150 cm) long.

2. Finish the fringe on both ends of the scarf using necktie knots (see page 51). Refer to the project diagram below for details on creating the fringe.

Note: *When picking up the strands of yarn for weaving, make sure to alternate between rows of fur yarn and rows of smooth yarn.*

PROJECT DIAGRAM

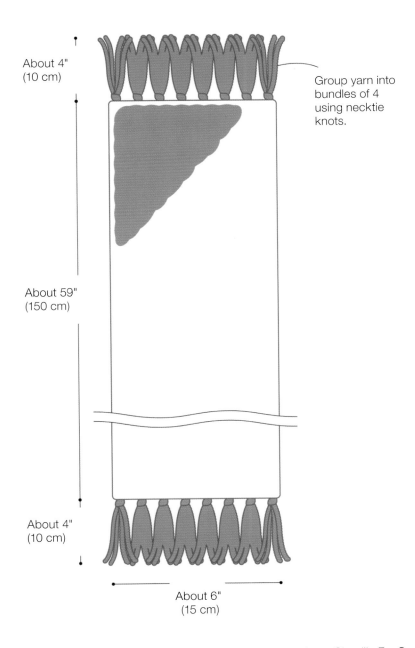

About 4"
(10 cm)

Group yarn into bundles of 4 using necktie knots.

About 59"
(150 cm)

About 4"
(10 cm)

About 6"
(15 cm)

Fiesta Fringe Shawl

Shown on page 15

MATERIALS

- 164 yards (556 g) of super bulky-weight (#6 super bulky) wool slub yarn in variegated pink/yellow
- 7 yards (7 g) of bulky-weight (#5 bulky) acrylic/wool blend smooth yarn in yellow
- 7 yards (7 g) of bulky-weight (#5 bulky) acrylic/wool blend smooth yarn in orange

GAUGE

- 7 weft yarns = 4" (10 cm)

GETTING STARTED

1. Cut 60 pieces of wool slub yarn that measure 98 ½" (250 cm) long each.

2. Attach the yarn to the ruler using the Single Knot Start Method (see page 33). Use 2 pieces of yarn for each bundle. Insert a string through for three rows to prevent your yarn from unraveling (see page 34).

Note: *This is a wide project that uses many strands of yarn. To make the weaving process easier, you can use the Center Start Method (see page 49).*

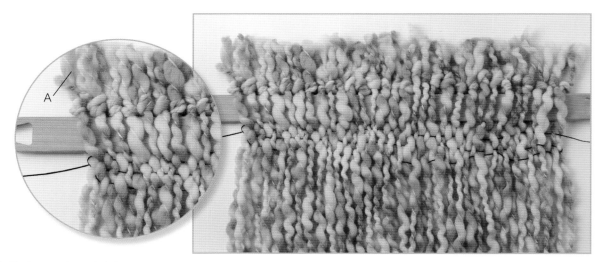

A: 2 pieces of wool slub yarn

INSTRUCTIONS

1. Weave using the Link Weaving Technique (see page 46) until the work measures 33 ½" (85 cm).

2. Finish the fringe on both ends of the scarf using necktie knots (see page 51) and coiled fringe (see page 54). Refer to the project diagram below for details on creating the fringe.

Note: *Weave tightly as this technique tends to produce a loose weave.*

PROJECT DIAGRAM

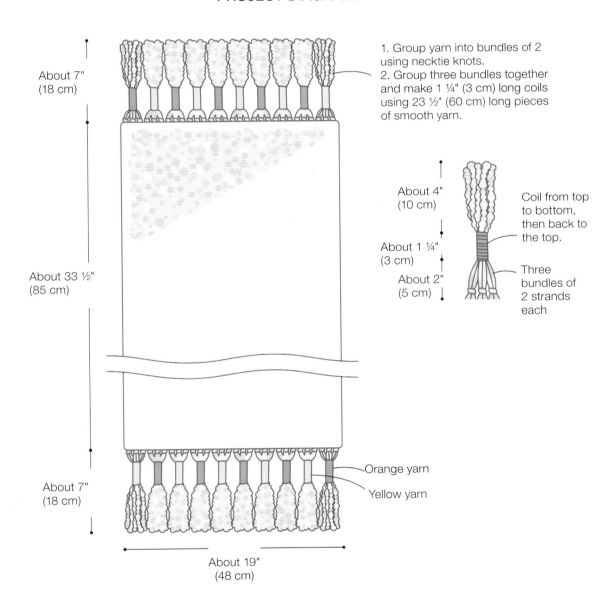

About 7" (18 cm)

About 33 ½" (85 cm)

About 7" (18 cm)

1. Group yarn into bundles of 2 using necktie knots.
2. Group three bundles together and make 1 ¼" (3 cm) long coils using 23 ½" (60 cm) long pieces of smooth yarn.

About 4" (10 cm)

About 1 ¼" (3 cm)

About 2" (5 cm)

Coil from top to bottom, then back to the top.

Three bundles of 2 strands each

Orange yarn

Yellow yarn

About 19" (48 cm)

Stashbuster Scarf

Shown on page 16

MATERIALS

- 328 yards (150 g) of worsted-weight (#4 medium) wool/acrylic blend yarn in red
- 197 yards (90 g) of worsted-weight (#4 medium) wool/acrylic blend yarn in maroon
- 66 yards (30 g) of worsted-weight (#4 medium) wool/acrylic blend yarn in green
- 66 yards (30 g) of worsted-weight (#4 medium) wool/acrylic blend yarn in blue
- 24 small rubber bands

GAUGE

- 4 weft yarns = 4" (10 cm)

GETTING STARTED

1. Combine 5 strands of red yarn, 3 strands of maroon yarn, 1 strand of blue yarn, and 1 strand of green yarn and roll into a ball to create multiple strand yarn.

2. Cut 24 pieces of multiple strand yarn that measure 98 ½" (250 cm) long each. Use rubber bands to hold each 10 strand piece together.

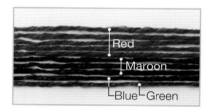

Multiple strand yarn ratio

3. Attach the yarn to the ruler using the Single Knot Start Method (see page 33). Use 4 pieces of multiple strand yarn for each bundle. Insert a string through for three rows to prevent your work from unraveling (see page 34).

A: 4 pieces of multiple strand yarn

INSTRUCTIONS

1. Weave using the Basic Weaving Technique (see page 37) until the work measures 55" (140 cm) long.

2. Finish the fringe on both ends of the scarf using necktie knots (see page 51). Refer to the project diagram below for details on creating the fringe.

Note: *When weaving, pick up each bundle by gripping the rubber band (see page 41).*

PROJECT DIAGRAM

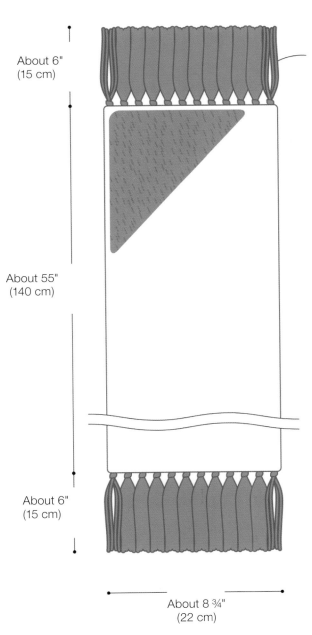

About 6" (15 cm)

Group 2 bundles of yarn together using necktie knots (just use one strand of yarn when tying the necktie knot).

About 55" (140 cm)

About 6" (15 cm)

About 8 ¾" (22 cm)

Cat Nap Lap Blanket

Shown on page 17

MATERIALS

- 105 yards (48 g) of worsted-weight (#4 medium) wool/acrylic blend yarn in red
- 112 yards (51 g) of worsted-weight (#4 medium) wool/acrylic blend yarn in maroon
- 525 yards (240 g) of worsted-weight (#4 medium) wool/acrylic blend yarn in green
- 322 yards (147 g) of worsted-weight (#4 medium) wool/acrylic blend yarn in blue
- 48 small rubber bands

GAUGE

- 4 weft yarns = 4" (10 cm)

GETTING STARTED

1. Separate 7 yards (7 m) each of maroon and blue yarn to be used for coiling the fringe once the weaving is complete.

2. Combine 5 strands of green yarn, 3 strands of blue yarn, 1 strand of red yarn, and 1 strand of maroon yarn and roll into a ball to create multiple strand yarn.

2. Cut 48 pieces of multiple strand yarn that measure 78 ¾" (200 cm) long each. Use rubber bands to hold each 10 strand piece together.

3. Attach the yarn to the ruler using the Single Knot Start Method (see page 33). Use 2 pieces of multiple strand yarn for each bundle. Insert a string through for three rows to prevent your work from unraveling (see page 34).

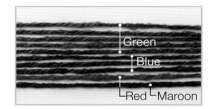

Multiple strand yarn ratio

A: 2 pieces of multiple strand yarn

INSTRUCTIONS

1. Weave using the Link Weaving Technique (see page 46) until the work measures 25 ½" (65 cm).

2. Finish the fringe on both ends of the scarf using necktie knots (see page 51) and coiled fringe (see page 54). Refer to the project diagram below for details on creating the fringe.

PROJECT DIAGRAM

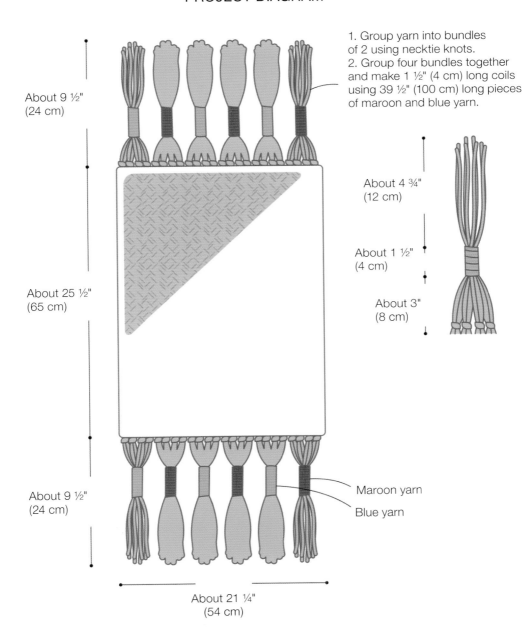

1. Group yarn into bundles of 2 using necktie knots.
2. Group four bundles together and make 1 ½" (4 cm) long coils using 39 ½" (100 cm) long pieces of maroon and blue yarn.

About 9 ½" (24 cm)

About 25 ½" (65 cm)

About 9 ½" (24 cm)

About 21 ¼" (54 cm)

About 4 ¾" (12 cm)

About 1 ½" (4 cm)

About 3" (8 cm)

Maroon yarn

Blue yarn

Cross Weave Neck Warmer

Shown on page 18

MATERIALS

- 40 yards (75 g) of super bulky-weight (#6 super bulky) wool yarn in mint green

GAUGE

- 4 weft yarns = 4" (10 cm)

GETTING STARTED

1. Cut 12 pieces of yarn that measure 118 ¼" (300 cm) long each.

2. Attach the yarn to the ruler using the Loop Start Method (see page 32). Once the yarn is attached to the ruler, there will be 24 strands of yarn that measure 59" (150 cm) long each. Insert a string through for three rows to prevent your work from unraveling (see page 34).

A: 1 piece of wool yarn

INSTRUCTIONS

1. Weave using the Cross Weaving Technique (see page 43) until the work measures 31 ½" (80 cm) long.
2. Finish the end fringe using necktie knots (see page 51) and the beginning fringe using the Braided Loop (see page 52). Refer to the project diagram below for details on creating the fringe.

PROJECT DIAGRAM

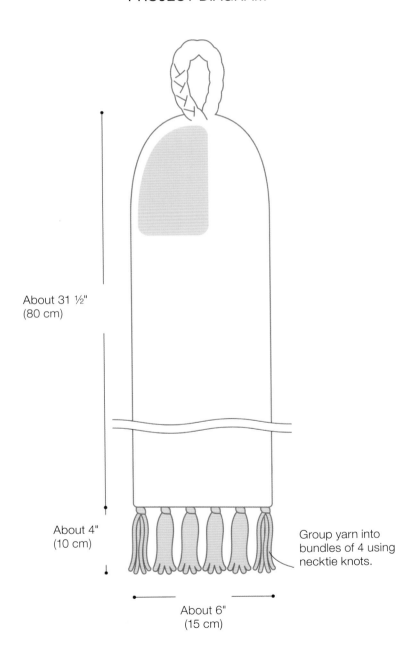

About 31 ½"
(80 cm)

About 4"
(10 cm)

Group yarn into
bundles of 4 using
necktie knots.

About 6"
(15 cm)

Cross Weave Purse

Shown on page 18

MATERIALS

- 64 yards (121 g) of super bulky-weight (#6 super bulky) wool yarn in mint green
- One set of 5 ¾" x 7 ¾" (14.5 x 19.5 cm) wicker handles

GAUGE

- 6 weft yarns = 4" (10 cm)

GETTING STARTED

1. Cut 48 pieces of yarn that measure 47 ¼" (120 cm) long each.

2. Attach 24 pieces of yarn to each handle using the Loop Start Method (see page 32). Once the yarn is attached to the handle, there will be 48 strands of yarn that measure 23 ¾" (60 cm) long each.

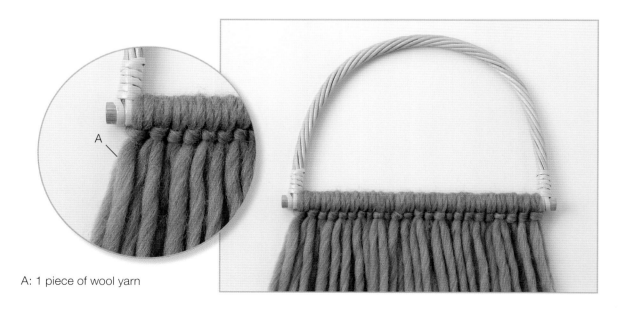

A: 1 piece of wool yarn

INSTRUCTIONS

1. Starting with the yarn attached to the first handle, weave using the Cross Weaving Technique (see page 43) until the work measures 11 ¾" (30 cm) long. Level out the end of the work as shown in step 10 on page 45. Follow the same process for the yarn attached to the second handle.

2. Layer the two woven pieces on top of each other. Join the two pieces together at the bottom using necktie knots (see page 51). Use 2 strands from each piece to tie each necktie knot.

3. Once all the necktie knots are complete, group them together in bundles of two. Coil the knots together using one of the 8 strands from the bundles (see page 54). When coiling, wrap the yarn 5 times.

4. Sew the sides of the purse closed using a scrap of yarn. Do not stitch all the way to the top to allow the bag to open.

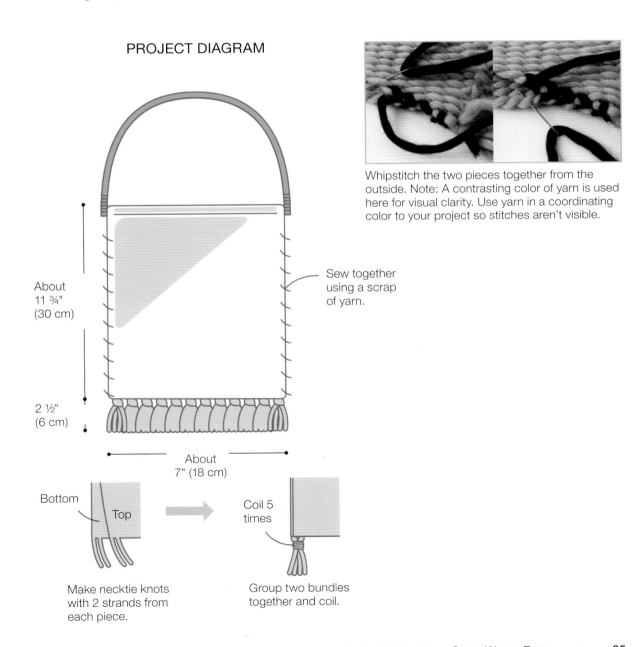

PROJECT DIAGRAM

Whipstitch the two pieces together from the outside. Note: A contrasting color of yarn is used here for visual clarity. Use yarn in a coordinating color to your project so stitches aren't visible.

About
11 ¾"
(30 cm)

Sew together
using a scrap
of yarn.

2 ½"
(6 cm)

About
7" (18 cm)

Bottom

Top

Coil 5
times

Make necktie knots
with 2 strands from
each piece.

Group two bundles
together and coil.

Classic Argyle Shawl

Shown on page 19

MATERIALS

- 44 yards (46 g) of super bulky-weight (#6 super bulky) wool/acrylic blend yarn in white
- 132 yards (137 g) of super bulky-weight (#6 super bulky) wool/acrylic blend yarn in pink
- 44 yards (46 g) of super bulky-weight (#6 super bulky) wool/acrylic blend yarn in blue
- 44 yards (46 g) of super bulky-weight (#6 super bulky) wool/acrylic blend yarn in brown

GAUGE

- 9 weft yarns = 4" (10 cm)

GETTING STARTED

1. Cut 48 pieces of pink yarn that measure 98 ½" (250 cm) long each. Cut 16 pieces each of white, blue, and brown yarn that measure 98 ½" (250 cm) long each.

2. Attach the yarn to the ruler using the Single Knot Start Method (see page 33). Use 6 pieces of yarn for each bundle. Refer to the photo below for yarn color order. Insert a string through for three rows to prevent your yarn from unraveling (see page 34).

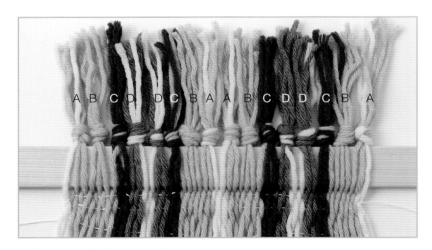

A: 2 pieces of white yarn + 4 pieces of pink yarn
B: 6 pieces of pink yarn
C: 4 pieces of brown yarn + 2 pieces of pink yarn
D: 4 pieces of blue yarn + 2 pieces of white yarn

INSTRUCTIONS

1. Weave using the Link Weaving Technique (see page 46) until the work measures 50 ½" (128 cm).
2. Finish the fringe on both ends of the scarf by twisting (see page 55). Refer to the project diagram below for details on creating the fringe.

Make sure to tighten the weave as you separate the two layers of yarn. This is very important for projects that use several strands of yarn.

PROJECT DIAGRAM

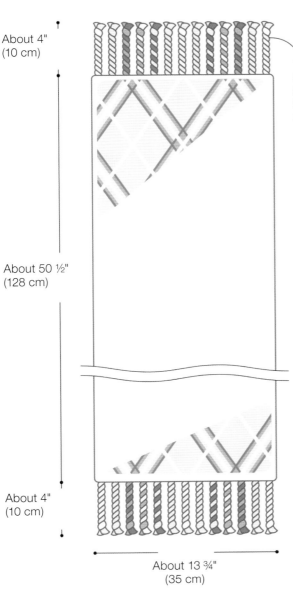

About 4"
(10 cm)

1. Twist 2 or 4 strands of the same colored yarn together.
2. Twist two twisted bundles together and secure with a necktie knot (see page 51).

About 50 ½"
(128 cm)

Note: *This is a wide project that uses many strands of yarn. To make the weaving process easier, you can use the Center Start Method (see page 49).*

About 4"
(10 cm)

About 13 ¾"
(35 cm)

Midnight Sky Stole

Shown on page 20

MATERIALS

- 132 yards (100 g) of bulky-weight (#5 bulky) acrylic/wool blend bouclé novelty yarn in variegated black
- 66 yards (19 g) of sport-weight (#2 fine) wool/nylon blend metallic yarn in black
- 66 yards (68 g) of bulky-weight (#5 bulky) wool/acrylic blend smooth yarn in navy
- 66 yards (68 g) of bulky-weight (#5 bulky) wool/acrylic blend smooth yarn in black
- 24 small rubber bands

GAUGE

- 4 weft yarns = 4" (10 cm)

GETTING STARTED

1. Combine 2 strands of variegated black bouclé yarn, 1 strand of black metallic yarn, and 1 strand each of navy and black smooth yarn and roll into a ball to create multiple strand yarn.

2. Cut 24 pieces of multiple strand yarn that measure 98 ½" (250 cm) long each. Use rubber bands to hold each 5 strand piece together.

3. Attach the yarn to the ruler using the Single Knot Start Method (see page 33). Use 2 pieces of multiple strand yarn for each bundle. Insert a string through for three rows to prevent your work from unraveling (see page 34).

A: 2 pieces of multiple strand yarn

Multiple strand yarn ratio

INSTRUCTIONS

1. Weave using the Cross Weaving Technique (see page 43) until the work measures 63" (160 cm). Weave the weft yarns into V shapes at both ends of the stole using the same process used in step 10 on page 45 (this will create a pointed V shape when starting from a level end).

2. Finish the fringe on both ends of the stole using necktie knots (see page 51). Refer to the project diagram below for details on creating the fringe.

PROJECT DIAGRAM

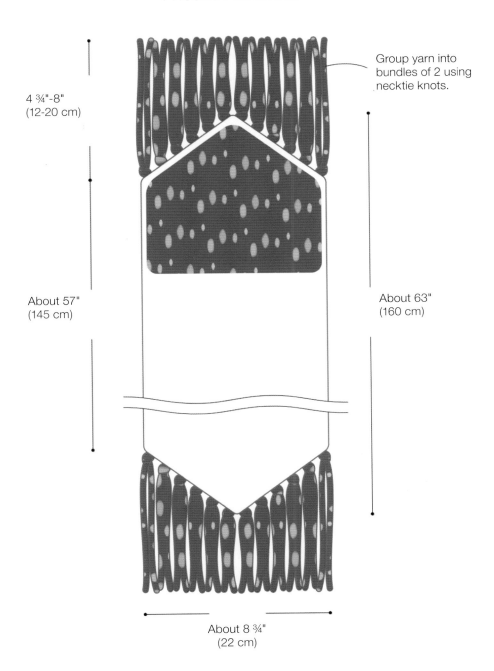

Group yarn into bundles of 2 using necktie knots.

4 ¾"-8" (12-20 cm)

About 57" (145 cm)

About 63" (160 cm)

About 8 ¾" (22 cm)

Beaded Bouclé Scarf

Shown on page 21

MATERIALS

- 70 yards (69 g) of bulky-weight (#5 bulky) wool/alpaca blend bouclé yarn in gray
- 100-120 beads in shades of pink and white

GAUGE

- 12 weft yarns = 4" (10 cm)

GETTING STARTED

1. Cut 32 pieces of yarn that measure 78 ¾" (200 cm) long each.

2. Attach the yarn to the ruler using the Single Knot Start Method (see page 33). Use 4 pieces of yarn for each bundle. Insert a string through for three rows to prevent your work from unraveling (see page 34).

3. Thread 10-12 randomly colored beads onto every third strand of yarn. When completed, there should be beads on 10 strands of yarn.

A: 4 pieces of bouclé yarn

It may be helpful to use a needle to thread the beads onto the yarn.

Note: *All beads in this photo are dark pink for visual clarity. Use beads in a variety of shades.*

INSTRUCTIONS

1. Weave using the Cross Weaving Technique (see page 43) until the work measures 41 ½" (105 cm). Make sure to evenly disperse the beads as you weave.

2. Level out the end of the work (see page 45). Finish the fringe on both ends of the scarf with braids (see page 56). Refer to the project diagram below for details on creating the braids.

Arrange beads as desired while weaving. They will be secured in place by the weft yarns.

PROJECT DIAGRAM

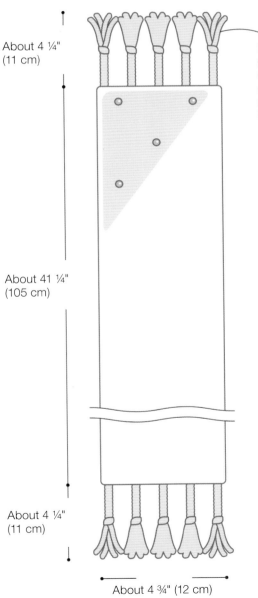

About 4 ¼" (11 cm)

Divide the yarn into five groups with 6-7 strands each. Form each group into a 2 ½" (6 cm) long braid and secure with a necktie knot (see page 51).

About 41 ¼" (105 cm)

About 4 ¼" (11 cm)

About 4 ¾" (12 cm)

Sweet Summer Scarves

Shown on page 22

MATERIALS

Wide Variation
- 66 yards (78 g) of bulky-weight (#5 bulky) cotton/nylon blend tape yarn in light blue

Narrow Variation
- 44 yards (52 g) of bulky-weight (#5 bulky) cotton/nylon blend tape yarn in blue

GAUGE
- 8 weft yarns = 4" (10 cm)

GETTING STARTED

1. For the wide variation, cut 24 pieces of yarn that measure 98 ½" (250 cm) long each. For the narrow variation, cut 16 pieces of yarn that measure 98 ½" (250 cm) long each.

2. Attach the yarn to the ruler using the Single Knot Start Method (see page 33). Use 4 pieces of yarn for each bundle. Insert a string through for three rows to prevent your work from unraveling (see page 34).

Wide Variation

A = 4 pieces of tape yarn

Narrow Variation

A = 4 pieces of tape yarn

INSTRUCTIONS

1. Weave using the Cross Weaving Technique (see page 43) until the work measures 57" (145 cm) long for the wide variation and 59" (150 cm) long for the narrow variation. Weave the weft yarns into V shapes at both ends of the scarf using the same process used in step 10 on page 45 (this will create a pointed V shape when starting from a level end).

2. Finish the fringe on both ends of the scarf using necktie knots (see page 51). Refer to the project diagrams below for details on creating the fringe.

> **Note:** *Lacy tape yarn folds and twists easily. Make sure to keep the width of the yarn even by adjusting the tightness of the weft yarn as you weave.*

PROJECT DIAGRAMS

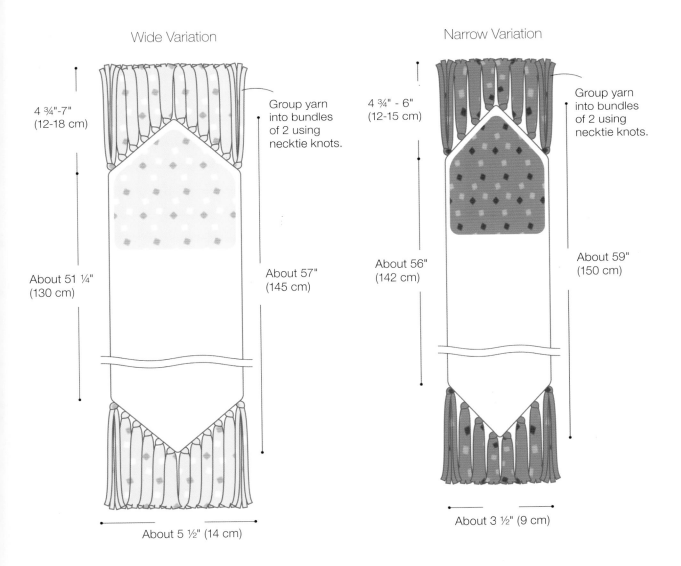

Wide Variation

4 ¾"-7" (12-18 cm)

Group yarn into bundles of 2 using necktie knots.

About 51 ¼" (130 cm)

About 57" (145 cm)

About 5 ½" (14 cm)

Narrow Variation

4 ¾" - 6" (12-15 cm)

Group yarn into bundles of 2 using necktie knots.

About 56" (142 cm)

About 59" (150 cm)

About 3 ½" (9 cm)

Striped Sunset Afghan

Shown on page 23

MATERIALS

- 97 yards (245 g) of bulky-weight (#5 bulky) mohair/nylon blend tube yarn in variegated orange/green
- 27 yards (67 g) of bulky-weight (#5 bulky) wool/nylon blend tube yarn in white

GAUGE

- 4 weft yarns = 4" (10 cm)

GETTING STARTED

1. Cut 44 pieces of variegated orange/green tube yarn and 12 pieces of white tube yarn that measure 78 ¾" (200 cm) long each. You should have a total of 56 pieces of yarn.

2. Attach the yarn to the ruler using the Single Knot Start Method (see page 33). Use 2 pieces of yarn for each bundle. Refer to the photo below for yarn color order. Insert a string through for three rows to prevent your work from unraveling (see page 34).

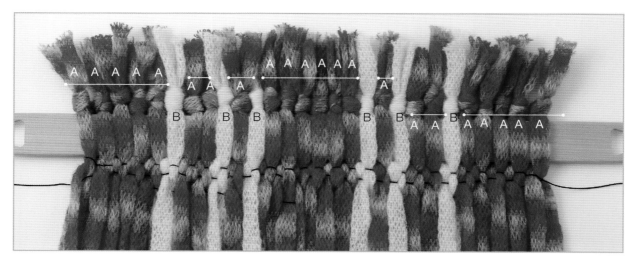

A: 2 pieces of orange/green variegated tube yarn
B: 2 pieces of white tube yarn

INSTRUCTIONS

1. Weave using the Basic Weaving Technique (see page 37) until the work measures 47 ¼" (120 cm) long.

2. Finish the fringe on both ends of the scarf using necktie knots (see page 51). Refer to the project diagram below for details on creating the fringe.

PROJECT DIAGRAM

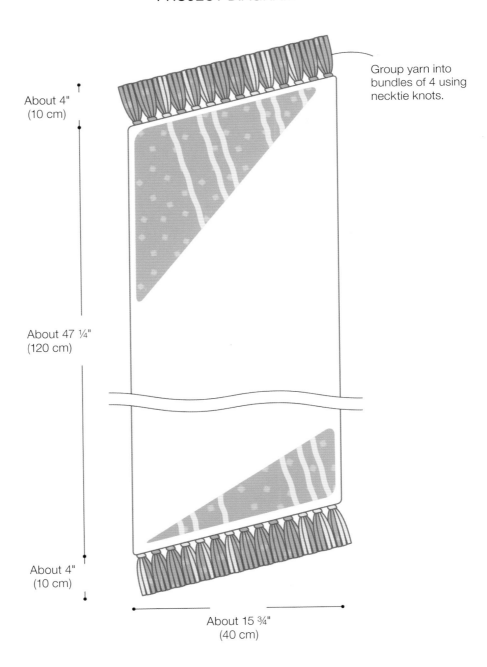

Group yarn into bundles of 4 using necktie knots.

About 4" (10 cm)

About 47 ¼" (120 cm)

About 4" (10 cm)

About 15 ¾" (40 cm)

Textured Lattice Scarf

Shown on page 24

MATERIALS

- 18 yards (40 g) of super bulky-weight (#6 super bulky) wool/acrylic blend faux fur chenille yarn in brown
- 70 yards (73 g) of bulky-weight (#5 bulky) wool/acrylic blend smooth yarn in white

GAUGE

- 10 weft yarns (2 fur strands + 8 smooth strands) = 4" (10 cm)

GETTING STARTED

1. Cut 8 pieces of faux fur chenille yarn and 32 pieces of smooth yarn that measure 78 ¾" (200 cm) long each.

2. Attach the yarn to the ruler using the Single Knot Start Method (see page 33). Use 2 pieces for the fur yarn bundles and 4 pieces for the smooth yarn bundles. Refer to the photo below for yarn color order. Insert a string through for three rows to prevent your yarn from unraveling (see page 34).

A: 2 pieces of faux fur chenille yarn
B: 4 pieces of smooth yarn

INSTRUCTIONS

1. Weave using the Link Weaving Technique (see page 46) until the work measures 39 ½" (100 cm).
2. Finish the fur yarn fringe on both ends of the shawl using necktie knots (see page 51). Finish the smooth yarn fringe on both ends of the shawl by twisting (see page 55). Refer to the project diagram below for details on creating the fringe.

Note: *As you weave, make sure the smooth yarn diamonds are equal in size.*

PROJECT DIAGRAM

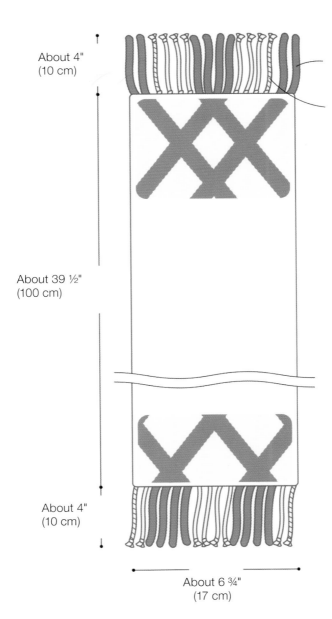

About 4"
(10 cm)

About 39 ½"
(100 cm)

About 4"
(10 cm)

About 6 ¾"
(17 cm)

Group fur yarn into bundles of 2 using necktie knots.

1. Twist 2 strands of smooth yarn together.
2. Twist two twisted bundles together and secure with a necktie knot.

Weaving Pattern Guide

You can create a variety of classic weaving patterns based on the order in which you attach the yarn to the ruler when getting started. Use this guide as a resource when designing your own projects. Note: These examples use 12 pieces of yarn attached to the ruler using the Loop Start Method (see page 32). This means that there will be 24 strands of yarn once attached to the ruler.

BASIC WEAVING TECHNIQUE

Attach 6 pieces of color A, then 6 pieces of color B.

This will create a thick, 6 strand striped pattern.

Attach 3 pieces of color A, then 3 pieces of color B. Repeat with remaining yarn.

This will create a thinner, 3 strand striped pattern.

Alternate colors every piece of yarn.

This will create a thin, vertically striped pattern. This method is used for the Basic Weaving Technique overview on page 37.

Alternate colors every piece of yarn. When inserting the string through to prevent your work from unraveling, align the strands as shown in the photo so they alternate colors.

This will create a border pattern that alternates colors for each row.

CROSS WEAVING TECHNIQUE

Attach 6 pieces of color A, then 6 pieces of color B.

Attach 3 pieces of color A, 6 pieces of color B, then 3 more pieces of color A.

This will create a zigzag pattern.

This will create a herringbone pattern. This method is used for the Herringbone Shawl on page 7.

LINK WEAVING TECHNIQUE

Attach 1 piece of color A, 3 pieces of color B, 3 pieces of color A, 3 pieces of color B, and 1 piece of color A. Attach a single strand of color A to each end using the Single Knot Start Method (see page 33), so there are 3 strands of color A on each end.

Attach 2 pieces of color A at the center, then alternate colors on each side as shown in the photo.

This will create a thinner checkered pattern compared to the Checkered Scarf on page 8.

This will create a wickerwork pattern.

Resources

CLOVER

Manufacturer of craft notions, including bias tape cutting rulers,
cutting mats, rotary cutters, rulers and scissors
http://www.clover-usa.com

JO-ANN FABRICS

National craft store selling yarn, fabric, beads, and other notions
http://www.joann.com

MICHAELS

National craft store selling yarn, beads, and other notions
http://www.michaels.com

WEBS

Wide selection of yarn, including novelty yarns, plus fringe
twisters and other fiber craft notions
http://www.yarn.com

Index

About the Author

*B*orn in Tokyo, Naoko Minowa studied home economics in college and graduated with a degree in dyeing. In 2011, she opened Studio A Week, a hand weaving and vegetable dyeing shop, school, and gallery. Naoko introduced the concept of finger weaving to provide her students with a friendly way to learn weaving. She is the author of many books and is the chairwoman of the Japan Senshoku Association, which celebrates the traditional Japanese art form of fabric dyeing.